Praise for *Finders*

"Every once in a while a million-dollar book is written—a book so full of wisdom that it could only have been written by a successful practitioner. *Finders Keepers* is such a book. If you make decisions about recruitment, selection or retention, the seasoned knowledge in *Finders Keepers* might be worth its weight in microchips. And you know what? It is also a fun read."

> Stephen C. Lundin, Big Tuna Ph.D.
> Author, *FISH! A Remarkable Way to Boost Morale and Improve Results*

"It's pretty rare that a business book makes you both think and smile. Russ Riendeau has made a career of doing that in person, and his endless supply of bite-sized wisdom transfers incredibly well to the page. You will dog-ear this thing to death."

> Ron Lieber, Senior writer
> *Fast Company* Magazine
> Author, *Upstart Start-Ups*

"Sixteen years of recruiting top sales talent for CEOs of established companies and high-flying entrepreneurs has taught Russ Riendeau a lot about finding the right salespeople...and keeping them! He shares his hard-won secrets in an easy-to-enjoy style. Use his secrets to make your sales organization the best it can be."

> Scott Pemberton, Publisher
> The Edward Lowe Report

"Russell Riendeau puts a real-world spin on tried-and-true practices for today's hiring managers and throws in enough innovative ideas to challenge the most seasoned managers."

Robert Mikesell, Founder and Partner
First Interview Network

"To help you win the war on talent, here's a sound, practical book with bite-sized pieces of advice to help you recruit and retain talented salespeople. A must-read for all sales managers!"

Jerome A. Colletti, Partner
Colletti-Fiss, LLC
Coauthor, *Compensating New Sales Roles* (AMACOM 2001)

"Check your assumptions at the door about how to have the best sales force. This is your blueprint for bringing the best on board."

Jack Altschuler, Chair
TEC, An International Organization of CEOs

"Efficient, affirming, inspiring, practical advice for architects of profit."

Noel Kreicker, President
IOR Global Services

Finders Keepers

Attracting and Retaining Top Sales Professionals

Russell J. Riendeau

Addicus Books, Inc.
Omaha, Nebraska

An Addicus Nonfiction Book

ISBN 1-886039-57-7
Cover design by George Foster
Typography by Linda Dageforde
Author photo by John Backe

Library of Congress Cataloging-in-Publication Data

Riendeau, Russell.
  Finders keepers : attracting and retaining top sales professionals / Russell J. Riendeau.
    p. cm.
  "An Addicus nonfiction book."
  ISBN 1-886039-57-7 (alk. paper)
  1. Employees—Recruiting. 2. Sales management. 3. Sales personnel.
I. Title.
  HF5549.5.R44 R535 2001
  658.3'044—dc21   2001001879

Addicus Books, Inc.
P.O. Box 45327
Omaha, Nebraska 68145
Web site: http://www.AddicusBooks.com
Printed in the United States of America
10 9 8 7 6 5 4 3 2 1

To Peter Bianchini, cofounder of Lexington Homes and creative vision behind Royal Oak Farm Orchard. His quiet accountability to the community, living in faith, giving more than an honest day's work, and believing each person has a gift to share, have contributed to the success of more individuals than we will ever realize.

Other books by Russell Riendeau

Thinking on Your Seat—A Catalyst to Create Respect, Results, and Revenue

Contents

Foreword

During an on-line sales chat recently, someone asked me for my opinion on sales books. My response, being a slow typist trying to say something in the fewest words, was "too many and too long." As a penance for some crime in a former life, I get sent dozens of new sales books every year and I feel compelled to read each one conscientiously. If I get a single good idea out of the average sales book it makes my day, but more often than not I come away wondering why I invested so much time to read a repackaging of the same old stuff. So, I must confess that when Russ Riendeau asked me to read the manuscript of *Finders Keepers*, my initial response was that sinking "here we go again" feeling.

But, for once, I was wrong. Within minutes of opening the book, I was engrossed and in little more than an hour I'd read it cover to cover. It has two great virtues:

Finders Keepers has a different perspective.

There are books on how to select salespeople. There are books on how to train them and how to compensate them. But nobody has written anything about how to keep them. Yet ask any successful senior sales manager about the secret of his or her success and you're likely to hear "I managed to keep the best performers." In this day and age, when top salespeople are at a premium and specialist headhunters lurk with tempting offers, keeping your top people is a real challenge. And there's very little in the way of helpful advice on how to do it except "pay them more." *Finders Keepers* provides a valuable and practical approach to retention of top talent and it deserves to succeed for that alone.

Finders Keepers **is commendably concise.**

Why do books on sales have to be so long-winded? Most sales managers I know are desperately overworked. If they have time to read books at all, they usually skim them, hoping for the occasionally useful idea. My way of judging business books is Rackham's Ratio: the number of practical ideas for every 1,000 words of prose. *Finders Keepers* scores well on both elements of the ratio. It has ideas—lots of them—and practical ones at that. And it's splendidly short and sharp with no unnecessary padding.

So let me not add superfluous prose either, but invite you to read, enjoy, and learn from this useful contribution to sales management success.

Neil Rackham
Chairman, Sales Strategy Institute
Author, *SPIN Selling*

Acknowledgments

I wish to express my gratitude to several individuals who helped turn this project from an "idea folder" into a printed book. I thank my friends and business colleagues who reviewed this manuscript, assuring applicability and accuracy. Your examples of professional and innovative business practices are a part of this book.

I especially thank Susan Adams, senior editor, for her encouragement, feedback and the gift of helping make my work a better book. I thank Rod Colvin of Addicus Books, my publisher, for his commitment to the project.

I'd like to express my appreciation to Lyle Stenfors and Tom Beamer for their creative input, and to Moe Ross for gentle reminders to follow the road less traveled.

To my wife Cheryl and our children, life is easier with your love and support.

Introduction

As a sixteen-year veteran executive recruiter, with nearly ten years of sales and management experience, I have been privileged to work with hundreds of the brightest and most innovative individuals in this country. Individuals who run major corporations, CEOs of mid-size companies, some of the highest-paid sales professionals, as well as young entrepreneurs looking to create the next juggernaut corporation.

Having witnessed their creative approaches to attracting and retaining potential managers and sales professionals, I've seen what has worked well and what has failed miserably. I have interviewed more than 25,000 individuals who have stayed with the firms for long-tenured careers, and I have spoken with those who bailed out quickly. The world of executive search is a virtual laboratory for observing human behavior and motivation.

The provocative, curious, and challenging ideas and strategies I'd like to share with you in *Finders Keepers* are all based on fundamental business principles. And as ludicrous as it sounds, the ideas are ripe with paradoxes of business practices that continually beg the mold to be broken, repaired, and broken again. What works yesterday won't work tomorrow. What motivates you will not motivate me. Your view of the world is exactly the same as mine in some ways and yet diametrically opposed in other aspects. This is the way the world has always been and will continue to be. What's important for you is to continue to experiment with approaches toward growing, maintaining, and enhancing your people skills. Just as critical is your ability to champion these concepts and beliefs to your business partners, employees, and family.

You may be a manager who makes hiring decisions; a CEO who is looking to impact your organization with fresh, dynamic change; a business owner seeking innovative ways to retain personnel; a sales professional who desires a management position. Whatever your situation, start today making changes in simple ways to win the game of *Finders Keepers.*

Section I

Attracting Top Talent:
The Coolest Magnet Wins

People come and go so quickly here...
—Dorothy, *The Wizard of Oz*

Sell the thunder.
They'll buy the rain.

Potential is what individuals look for in a new job.

I recently reviewed the past 100 placements my search firm made and found, amazingly enough, that more than 40 percent of these positions did not exist thirty-six months ago! Can you sell the opportunity to potential hires that they can define and create a new job for themselves? Even design a new commission plan to reward dynamic sales growth? Does your culture promote this entrepreneurial spirit? Selling thunder is easy: it's loud, demands attention, and has energy. But after you've heard it a few times you get used to it. But a steady, nurturing rain of support, freedom, and reward is what will attract the elite to your doorstep and keep them contributing to your profits and their portfolios.

"...I love you, Danny, but I can't marry you...It's the pigs."

from *Waking Ned Devine*

Check with a consultant to confirm your compensation plan ranks in your industry's 80th percentile. If not, change it.

In the quirky and hilarious film Waking Ned Devine, a small farming town in Ireland schemes to snooker the county out of the lottery winnings of a dead man. One of the stories in the film is the love between a pig farmer and a lady in town. She loves him but can't bring herself to marry him and live with the smell of a pig farm. Only when he gets the lottery dough and bids the farm adieu does she agree to marry him. Moral of the story: Why put your energy into convincing potential employees to join your firm when you don't pay a competitive wage?

Up the ante. Attract the better talent with better pay—not a lot more, but slightly more than the rest—just below the No.1 in your marketplace. See what happens. You'll reduce turnover (which will offset the cost increases of better pay plans), enhance morale, attract better talent, and rid yourself of making excuses. It also makes a bold statement to your customers that you want and expect the best. They won't object as much either when you raise your prices if you're doing a great job!

Hear ye, hear ye! A radical proclamation

*Announce and publish your policies, philosophy of
business practice, and hiring process to the world.*

Write a mission statement with an attitude, then post it
everywhere—from the lobby to the company newsletter to the back of pay stubs. Let potential employees know what your company is really about—its philosophy and business practices. Rarely do you see this coura-
geous approach to attracting new talent. All too often companies spend big bucks telling what they can do for the customer—the thousands of employees ready to help them, the
500 service centers armed with personnel. This is all well and
good, but it doesn't say anything about the philosophy of
customer service issues, freedom to make decisions, flexible
pay options for sales and service people. There is nary a
word about what good things will happen when an em
ployee works hard and smart, and what will happen if he or
she doesn't.

Be different! Let employees know how their hard work
will be rewarded. And announce up front and out loud
that employees will be fired if they don't do their work. A
few of the newer, innovative technology firms have caught
the wave and are benefitting from this candid and radically
refreshing approach to hiring. Be radical! Tell it like it is!

Don't negotiate with a plumber
on Christmas Eve.

Good talent is hard to find, and it ain't cheap.

A general manager told me a story about the time his wife attempted an Oriental noodle recipe on Christmas Eve for their guests. At her request, he tasted it. She wanted feedback, so he offered his assessment: "Yuck!" She immediately dumped the entire contents into the sink, taxing the poor garbage disposal and creating a seriously clogged pipe.

Close to 8:00 P.M. he finally found a plumber. "Gonna cost you double, you know!" the voice challenged. "Tell you what I'll do," said the general manager, "I'll pay you two and a half times your fee if you're here in thirty minutes!" The plumber came and fixed the drain. Money well spent.

Being cheap is a habit and one that won't serve you well if you're going after top talent. The American way of negotiation is: make an offer, other party counters, first party counters the counter, they agree to split the difference, and the deal is done. Attracting great people with this approach won't work. Why? Because the top performers in every market know this game. They play it every day with their customers. They're good at it and don't have to play with you. Make a solid offer and be prepared to pay a premium for the best. If you need a person to start yesterday, now is not the time to try to save money. Your customers are feeling the lack of attention, and it will be hard to replace them. Remember the lesson my general manager friend learned: the plumber doesn't *have* to come out to fix your drain on Christmas Eve—you've got to convince him he can't afford *not* to come.

"...and, this coffin makes a neat go-cart chassis if you decide not to use it below grade!"

Be creative in selling the benefits of working for your organization!

If you have a product a potential employee might think of as boring, sell the excitement of its application and who its customers are. Demonstrate to potential hires how your product contributes to the health of people, the impact on an industry, the new technology it holds, the future of the marketplace, the commission plan they will enjoy, the lack of strong competition in the arena, and so on. Show candidates there is more to the sale than what they think. Everybody needs to feel strongly about the product or service he or she sells, so help the individual to see the possibilities previously overlooked.

It's not always about the money.

*People change jobs for reasons
beyond the almighty and alluring buck.*

Your ability to attract top talent depends on your company's ability to be competitive in many arenas. In a survey a few years ago, a major corporation found that money was one of the top ten reasons people took jobs, but it wasn't number one. Other factors ahead of it included advancement potential, personal satisfaction, recognition (a feeling of worth and contribution), surroundings, professionalism, management style of their boss, commute time, and above-average pay for the work assignment. Money alone will not attract top talent. Ask candidates what factors will influence their decision to take or reject a job offer from you.

"Xanadu is over there, madam."

*Being candid with potential hires will go farther
in securing them for your organization.*

Most people realize no company is perfect. All businesses, unlike the mythical, magical place called Xanadu, must deal with public and private issues daily.

Each one has a unique cluster of issues, agendas, and pressures to face in an ever-changing market. Be candid with candidates. Explain in positive language what problems your company faces, what you're doing about them right now, and what you're planning to do in the future. Show them how they can contribute to the company to make it better. Show them where the ideas are coming from. And let them know they'll be asked for their suggestions if they become part of the team. Ask potential hires to offer a suggestion for improving the company's performance based on their observations.

If your firm has had bad press lately, discuss it openly and candidly. Defend, but don't sell. Explain the issue as it relates to the industry as a whole. A client of mine, an environmental cleanup company, was great at attracting talent from its larger competitors. Why? Because they promoted the fact that the industry had big problems as a whole, but by working for a smaller firm one could make a greater impact on fixing the problem. They emphasized the difficulties large, slow-moving corporations can have with an overly cautious board of directors too scared to make the wrong moves. And they did attract top-flight talent that did make a difference!

Brag about people who have left your company.

Admit it? YES!

B ragging about individuals who have left can demonstrate just how well you train people to be superstars. It shows up front that you hire the best talent possible. Letting candidates see that they may learn a lot more than they expected is essential to retaining top talent and being able to continually challenge them in their respective roles. This honest approach gives you the opportunity to show a mentoring attitude, helping them recognize that if they want to advance, they must help find their replacement and mentor that person. In reality, people don't like to change jobs. We all like to be part of a successful team or family. Find ways to show that people can grow, prosper, be challenged, and be recognized within your company. And if they outgrow their jobs, they know they'll be very marketable in the business world having worked for you. Who knows, they may leave, open a business, and hire you as CEO and partner!

Walk a mile in their shoes.

*Engage human resources personnel to work closely
with management in hiring sales professionals.
Get them out into the field.*

Arrange for your HR staff to spend some time in the field. As they learn what sales professionals are responsible for and with whom they deal every day, they will be better able to spot a qualified candidate in the sea of resumes and Internet bios. It will also give them freedom to consider alternative backgrounds. I know, as a professional recruiter, if I can spend some time with sales-people or managers from various departments, my success ratio goes way up when I'm looking for the right person for the job. More and more managers are mandating that recruiters spend time with more people in the company to provide a better picture of the culture and pace of the company.

May I take your order, please?

Written job descriptions are always required.

All too often hiring managers seek out a new person for a job without spending even thirty minutes composing a thoughtful job description. Writing down specific elements of the job—duties, activities, and goals—is the clearest method to determine whether the job sounds desirable, competitive in the marketplace, and attractive to persons who have met the criteria.

The job descriptions should include not only the duties and responsibilities found in the corporate manual, but also additional information to help potential employees decide whether the job will be a comfortable fit. Describe typical customers and their expectations, the kinds of negotiations the person will engage in, the culture of a typical client. Let the candidate know what traits are essential to being happy and successful in this role. Does the job require travel? Where are the customers now? Are they staying put? Will additional geography be added to the territory? What kind of reporting is required and how often? How detailed must it be? What does the training program outline look like? Does it include a history of the company? Pictures of the products made or services rendered? Is there formal classroom learning or baptism by fire? Is the company philosophy spelled out in simple words?

As you develop this additional information, ask yourself if you would come to work here if you heard what the candidate will be hearing. Be honest with yourself.

Don't be afraid to give a copy of this information to candidates during the interview and ask them to think it over and call you back in a day or so. Let them sleep on it, as you will about them fitting into the organization. This kind of forthright approach is disarming and respected by people who have been promised so much from firms, only to be burned.

Rapid reconnaissance to sharpen the image of your company

Three enlightening questions to ask every employee in the next week to validate your recruitment strategy:

- *What attracted you to this organization?*
- *What keeps you here?*
- *What concerns you enough to consider leaving?*

Ask these three questions through a confidential, no-names-anywhere questionnaire. Put this questionnaire into every paycheck envelope with a note from you stating why you're asking. To better the firm, naturally. Pure and simple.

Rapid reconnaissance, an expression coined by researchers means "to gather data quickly to assist in making changes in a policy, method, or position." The media uses this tactic with opinion polls on busy street corners, web site log-ons, and telephone polls. The data is quick, candid, and at times very ambiguous. However, it can provide insight and accurate feedback concerning hunches and observations. These three questions will elicit varying responses; some will baffle you, others will surprise you, and the rest will teach you. This immediate feedback will help direct how your firm presents itself to the candidate in interviews, advertisements, and web site design. Gather your staff with these comment cards and sort out the real issues from the inconveniences. And don't take any too lightly.

Encouraging them to find another job?
Well, sorta.

Parallel careers are here to stay. Embrace the benefits.

People who are energized enough to have a small business or a hobby turning a profit are typically bright, motivated people. The engineer who consults on the side, the plant manager who restores and sells antique cars, the marketing manager who builds doll furniture—all have talents they want to expand and share. To discourage a person from this will do more harm than good, and the individual may leave for a more understanding employer elsewhere. (The exception is the employee having an obvious conflict of interest or so much time away from the job that it becomes an issue.) Be open to unique ways people try to get ahead, plan for retirement, pay for nice vacations, and create niches in the business community. Maybe some of those ideas can filter into your organization.

Running help wanted ads with pizzazz!

Stuffy, boring ads draw stuffy, boring people.

Even with the growth of Internet job boards, professional recruiters, industry newsletters, and journals, the newspaper is still a quick, cheap, and effective way to spread the word that you have a job opening. The way to attract the talented sales and management persons reading the paper is through more creative ads. Rather than post the job's basic requirements in "blah" language, capture the reader's attention with questions like: Can you show me documented proof you're in the top 10 percent of the salespeople in your company? What awards have you won? What did you invent, write, create, fix, learn, discover, design, paint, sell, buy, or save that demonstrates you are better at the job than all the rest? What skills do you have that few others possess? What can you teach? Try these questions next time you need someone special. If the applicants can't provide documentation in the first sixty seconds of the interview, it's over—and they know it. They read the ad.

Section II

Who to Hire:
Chasing the Purple Squirrel

There is something that is much more scarce, something rarer than ability. It is the ability to recognize ability.
—Robert Half

Chasing the purple squirrel

A good salesperson can sell anything...is a myth.

When a new player in the copier industry ventured into the American market in the early 1980s they lured—with big signing bonuses and fat commission promises—the salespeople from established players like Xerox and IBM. It worked. The salespeople jumped ship for the new kid on the block, yet they failed miserably. Reason? The company discovered that the sales professionals selling a brand name product sold differently than those selling a "non-brand name" product. (Brand name products are those that are considered "household names." They have long histories of dependability, celebrity endorsements, and fancy advertising. Non-brand name products are sold around the concept "it's time for a change." These products offer new features, introductory pricing, and are often pitched as a backup to your existing product.) But, once management realized the old adage, "a good salesperson can sell anything" is a myth, they refocused recruitment efforts to secure successful sales professionals from non-brand name companies. Result: sales rocketed and that company is still in business today.

Chasing a purple squirrel refers to seeking an ideal

job candidate who, in reality, does not exist. No one person has all the attributes, experience, image, and price tag to fit a sales job profile.

The key is to seek out people who can relate to your industry's sales cycle, cost systems, delivery schedules, and manufacturing processes. If a person has experience and skills in an industry with similar practices, he or she should be able to adapt to your marketplace quickly. For example: a person selling for a local bank could understand the sale of financial services to corporations. A person in the hospitality sector could understand retail or even healthcare. Someone in the freight business could adapt to automotive, railroad or the aviation industry. I've even witnessed numerous individuals leave the field of politics, becoming successful sales directors and operations managers because of their talent and experience of building teams and consensus building. Look closer at what skills are really being used in a given job.

Hire the "renegades!"

If they have a trail of positive value to an organization or a history of shaking up the group, bring 'em on board!

Often, renegades don't get hired because the manager sees "high maintenance" written all over them. Oh well, that's why they pay you the big bucks to make it happen. If you find people who don't fit the mold, don't discount them right away. Look at what they've accomplished in their lifetime. Can their unique, or even quirky, skills be harnessed and channeled into your company? Can they teach you something you don't know? If they survived and received a paycheck from someone for years, they must be doing something productive. Dig deeper in your interviews. Do thorough reference checks to learn what style works in harnessing their talents. Have them meet other members of your staff, for they might spot the small diamond in the rough you're about to step over.

Hire personality, not just pedigree.

Reforest your organization with hardy seedlings.

G o into the corporate rest room and look yourself in the mirror. Would you have hired you when you were fresh out of school? Someone did. Why did they hire you? What spark, idea, attitude, energy did you exude to secure an offer without the experience they and everybody else said you needed to get hired? Those same traits are in others as well. Look closely for individuals with these qualities. They are out there!

Future billionaires wanted

Starting out, Microsoft's Bill Gates didn't run ads that read, "Must have Windows experience." Hire those with histories of past successes.

When you rewrite the job description, make an effort to describe the job without using the clichés of a basic job description. Express in action words what the job really is about, its core issues, what a person needs to like to do, and what he or she might dislike about the job. What kinds of customers will he or she call on? See if the traits and characteristics of the job match other industries as well, thus opening up a whole new arsenal of available talent you never considered.

Bring the mad scientists on board.

If they've survived in business this far, they must have talent. Find it and enhance it.

Mad scientists are different from renegades. You know renegades will be a handful from the get-go. The mad scientist types—you just don't know about. Young, inexperienced managers or managers lacking courage will always hire the "safe candidate" for a position. If the person doesn't work out, the manager won't be criticized for hiring him or her. But hiring a mad scientist will always raise the eyebrows of the "finger pointers" looking for you to screw up. Take a chance. Look deeper into people's nature and skills—beyond their wild hair, their theories of evolution, or the Hummer vehicles they pulled up in. They may have secret talents you need now.

Have you ever watched any television award shows? You get to see and hear the people behind the writing and creation of the most successful movies, plays, and TV programs. They never look and sound like you thought they would, or should, do they? If the person you're interviewing has been successful somewhere else, find out how and harness the talent. So what if he or she lives in a pyramid-shaped house and sleeps on pine cones.

Gold watches are for train conductors, not for today's sales elite.

Candidates today take different tracks to get to their destination. Those who show numerous jobs early in their career show a willingness to take risks and venture out.

The days of the gold watch ceremony for the twenty-year employee are dwindling. As our job market continues to evolve into a project-oriented/performance-based employment arena, the necessity for a person to demonstrate long tenures at companies is becoming less pronounced. The reality is that the person who has worked for three companies in fifteen years is more valuable and sought after than a person who has worked for one company for fifteen years. Why? That individual has a broader band of experience and proof he or she can adapt to change. What's important is when the person worked at these different positions and what he or she did while there. Quick job changes early in a post-college career are typically made out of naiveté, lack of direction, or a missing mentor.

Conversely, excessive jobs late in a career can show

confusion and a lack of updated skills. Experimenting with a few different jobs can be a great lesson before a person sets firm with a company for many years. If the individual doesn't investigate other opportunities early, he or she will likely be curious later. Spend adequate time exploring the person's real passions and successful experiences in life outside work as well. Herein lie clues to what the candidate may be searching for in a career.

Does the job seat cushion spring right back up?

Look deeper when interviewing sales professionals having more than six years with their current employer. Complacency and lack of motivation to excel could be present.

I have a favorite chair at home. If you were to sit in it, the chair would be uncomfortable. The cushions are now shaped to conform to my body, not yours. People stay in jobs with the same effect. Steady employment with one company is still looked upon as a positive. Loyalty and consistent performance are indeed important. However, if the long-tenured person has had the same job, has performed at the same level, has not grown sales substantially, and has been given only a few token promotions, then he or she is not the person you want to lead your group to the promised land.

If you need managers to implement change, be sure when interviewing to find out what they've been doing outside the workplace. Starting a family, getting an MBA, renovating houses, caring for a sick family member—all may show they have the drive to excel, but perhaps they haven't had the time or the opportunity to express it fully. Remember, loyalty and longevity are not same thing.

Talent is nature. Training is nurture.

*Constantly be in recruitment mode
to recognize talent in unusual places.*

As Peter Drucker states in *Management Challenges for the 21st Century,* in a low unemployment economy, coupled with an aging population, there is simply less talent to choose from. Sales and management talent are having strong years financially; consequently, their motives to change jobs can be difficult to assess. Some will change for a big, fat increase in income; others want the perks of a king. If you become good at assessing the talent *outside* your industry, you can build a more loyal team that won't change for only money. Remember, long ago you may not have had the experience you needed for a job you were hired for. Someone saw something in you that made him or her take a risk. And research shows that sales individuals coming from outside the industry will excel faster in sales goals, get promoted faster, and stay with your company longer.

Catch, release, and catch later.

Keep track of the upcoming Superheroes.

Clever managers are always recruiting and networking. What if you don't have any openings? Don't worry, you will. In the meantime, when you meet dynamic, young talent that still need some street-seasoning smarts, keep in touch with them, mentor them, encourage them, and guide them. Toss them back in the business-world pond and let them grow. Then put your pole in the water and reel them in for your business a year or two later. These young people are your future elite.

I won't go and you can't make me!

*The potential employee who is not willing
to relocate isn't all bad. This attitude shows a belief
in the community. This conviction can be
demonstrated and marketed to the customer.*

Blended families, aging parents in need of long-term health care from family and cost of living are all factors keeping people in their neighborhoods. Cultural differences across the country and the effort to adjust to them can also make it difficult for people to move, even for a great promotion. Allowing employees to remain local encourages loyalty and can even be good for business. Customers like dealing with a neighbor rather than a superstar on his way to another job.

Is it "broke" or doesn't it "work"?

*A technical degree doesn't guarantee
the ability to sell a technical product or service.
It means the person who earned it can understand
the process, not necessarily the prospect.*

What about the guy whose GPA was 1.8 out of 4.0 and still graduated as an engineer? Yikes! Some of the sharpest sales talent I've met are liberal arts majors and psychology majors. If the product features can be taught, don't hold out for an engineer to sell the product. There aren't that many engineers who like to sell in the first place, and sales personalities, in general, hold a high level of curious attitudes that shore up any technical deficiencies they may have. Many of the companies our firm has worked with avoid hiring individuals with engineering degrees because they're afraid the person will spend too much time on technical issues and too little time on selling and prospecting for new customers.

Consider hiring the No. 2 candidate.

No. 2 candidates can be the unsung heroes.

No. 2 sometimes is likable, but doesn't have as much "industry experience" as No. 1, so you pick number 1. If No. 1 is hard to pin down with an offer, shows signs of hesitancy in taking the job, makes unreasonable demands, or holds out for big bucks, hire No. 2. That person wants the job more, will take it for reasonable pay, and is less likely to defect to your competitor.

One stint at a dot-com is okay.

Life is about deciding levels of risk vs. reward.

If the resume of a potential candidate shows he or she worked for a now-defunct dot-com company, don't be too hard on him or her. The romance and allure of the Internet is compelling and is hard to say "no" to. Most have learned the hard way by seeing the company go out of business. This individual will be a smarter businessperson as a result of the experience.

Hire the disabled.

The power of the human spirit should never be underestimated.

Millions of Americans with disabilities hold down jobs, and they are darn good at what they do. Keep your eyes and ears open for such talent. These individuals are worth their weight in gold.

One percentage point shouldn't stop you from buying a house.

Don't wait for Mr. or Ms. Perfect to show up.
A little extra training of a solid candidate
will give you a superstar quicker than waiting
for one to magically appear.

A candidate with a solid personality, strong education, and readiness to change can outperform talent from your industry that has to be wooed or convinced to come to your company. Taking one month to train, read industry newsletters, and attend one trade show will get most inexperienced sales professionals up to speed. The minor details and technical assistance they can get from internal staff and you. Bottom line: Hire a solid person and don't wait for Mr. or Ms. Wonderful.

Section III

How to Hire:
Soup, Salad, and Tons of Questions

*A single conversation across the table with a wise man
is worth a month's study of books.*
—Chinese proverb

Sales candidate interview
question of the century

*"What businesses did you start from the time you were
eight years old through high school?"*

Entrepreneurs and leaders start early in their quest to
do something apart from the group. Find out what
they did. I worked with a VP of Sales who believed
that every sales professional or sales manager that was
above average in his or her profession started out early in
business pursuits. He probed in the interview to see who
shoveled snow from driveways, cut lawns, worked at the
grocery store, baby-sat, worked toward an Eagle Scout
Badge, or sold Girl Scout cookies. In college did they
work in the mess tent, paint houses in the summer, work
as lifeguards or make and sell T-shirts with the school logo
on the front? All these chances to earn a living show
gumption and a willingness to work hard. They also demonstrate a desire and drive to become independent of others, such as their parents. Test this theory out on your existing staff. Find out who was the most assertive in his or
her youth and see if that person is the most highly paid.

Listen...very carefully.

It's how they say it that can make the difference.

A good friend and CEO told me of a time he was interviewing a woman for a sales position with his firm. During the lunch interview, he was situated across from her and the sun was in his eyes, preventing him from seeing her face clearly. Rather than change tables, he sat and listened to her, discovering she had a captivating voice and energy. The job she was interviewing for required a lot of phone contact, and he knew she'd be fantastic with customers.

Too many times we are duped into believing image is more important than content. Words, passion, emotion, conviction, motivation, a history of success are far more critical than hiring image in an empty suit. Phone etiquette and energy are the big differences between an average sales professional and a superstar.

A good way to listen without the distraction of physical appearance is to speak with the candidate on the phone to see what impact the individual makes. The impression you get may more accurately indicate what he or she is really like. Attentive listening also shows genuine interest and respect for that person, further enhancing the candidate's opinion of you as a compassionate, professional manager.

Brown-bag lunch and a bus ride

Take all viable candidates on a field trip.

Anxiety is the word that best describes how people feel before accepting a new job. Fear of the unknown is a strong emotion that can be eased by letting the person see exactly what they're getting into. Have each candidate ride with you or a salesperson for a half a day, or spend time in the office, plant, or city he or she will be working in. Meet some customers, see the shop floor or service center, listen to people doing their jobs. This approach offers you a chance to see each candidate's reactions to the surrounding environment. Look for clues and evidence of interest, disinterest, boredom, or concern in their eyes. See what questions they ask. (If they don't ask any, look out!) If this field trip doesn't scare them away, offer them the job. If you see any signs of wavering interest, probe for problems and keep interviewing more candidates.

Read 'em like a book.

*Ask candidates what three books they've read
in the past year and what literature is
on their coffee table at home right now.*

A person who doesn't read is no better off than a person who can't read. What people read is a view into their heart, soul, and interests. A person who doesn't read at least one book a year is at a distinct disadvantage with customers in social visits or negotiating. Keeping current with world events, business trends, creative thinking, and psychology has a direct correlation to personal income. I recently interviewed a forty-six-year-old CPA/controller who admitted he's not read a business book or any writings about his field in the past twelve years. His income reflects his lack of skills update, and he is fearful of losing his job to a younger person. I wonder why? Reading and vocabulary are two signals to potential employers of the person's currency of skills and motivation to maintain a competitive edge in business.

CHOW CALL!

Meet with every sales candidate for hire at least three times, at different times and places each time. Watch them eat.

All of us have different peak energy times. Meeting a person once and deciding that the individual is not right for the job may be unfair—to you and to the candidate. If a person appears to have some potential but the "chemistry" isn't quite right, see the candidate again at another time of the day, and at a different location. People respond differently to the stress of a job interview. Some take longer to calm down or get more animated.

Think back to how you interact with others and give the candidate the benefit of the doubt if he or she is not perfect in the interview. Most people interview fewer than fifteen times during their business career, so no one should be smooth and flawless. If a potential employee is, it should be cause for concern. The act of dining out can show much about a person's social graces, health awareness, and conversation style. The event can be a great starter toward learning more about that person's lifestyle, goals, and other talents.

Dear John…

*Get a sample of any potential hire's writing skills
to verify an ability to communicate on paper.*

Just as the phone voice is critical, a person's ability to communicate on paper is vitally important. E-mail, memos, and letters written by remote sales professionals go out to customers without any proofreading. Are you willing to take the risk of unprofessional and embarrassing letters? Have a potential employee write a sample letter to a customer for you. Have him or her send you a sample of a proposal recently mailed out. Ask whether the candidate attended college and whether English was a strong or weak subject. A good assistant can shore up weak skills in this area, so if the person is strong in other areas, he or she is not totally out of the running. But get the new hire a good grammar book and a dictionary in a hurry!

On psychological assessments

Use tests to help you to manage and coach.
Do not use them as final decision-makers to determine
whom to hire. Reliance on assessment reports builds
weak interviewers and indecisive managers.

Assessment testing has reached an all-time high with the influx of Internet-based "quickie personality" profiles. But many of these tests do not have the validity and reliability factors to make them useful other than for curiosity's sake. Assessment profiles, even the best ones, should not be used exclusively to pick a winner. In a study of over 300 companies that I've worked with, I learned that about half don't use any kind of psychological assessment tools. Some studies have not shown major differences in performance issues, lower turnover rates, or more frequent promotions in companies that do assessments.

Dr. Jean Piaget, the world-renowned researcher in child psychology, did studies that tested genius in children. He found that if he changed the way the tests were presented—written form, verbal form, question and answer, essay—different segments of the group showed genius. In other words, different children were identified as geniuses using each of the different tests. The point is, people excel and learn by different methods, yet all have potential never tapped. Bottom line: Assessments are a great tool in interviewing. Use them as such without giving them the power of the final decision to hire or not. The key element that cannot be fully assessed is the potential of an inspired and motivated individual.

If you love lobster, you'll pay market price.

When you find who you need, pay for value.

It's Saturday night and you're out with your spouse for dinner. You'll pay whatever the amount to satisfy your craving for lobster. The same principle applies to the search for talent. Good talent is always more expensive. Pay the extra. Don't try to get sharp sales professionals with weak salary offers. They'll leave if a better offer comes along, or will resent your offer forever, even if they take the job. Giving a stronger commission plan with sales performance is better than giving nothing to someone who has sold nothing. It's like the buyer who tries to negotiate with a vendor after her "favorite" vendor can't deliver product. The buyer asks: "How much? Our other vendor sells it for five dollars per foot." The seller responds: "Then buy it from them!" Buyer: "They don't have any." Seller: "Well, when I don't have any, I sell it for one dollar per foot!" If you have salary parity issues that preclude your hiring a new employee for a bigger salary, even though the person is worth more than your existing talent, it's time to change the policy. You're penalizing yourself with mediocrity.

The definition of insanity

Doing the same thing over and over while expecting different results. Are you hiring a person who fits a mold, or someone who can make a difference?

The banking industry has always complained about how difficult it is to hire bank tellers. Why? Because the job doesn't pay that well. They also say it is the most important job because bank tellers meet the customers all the time. Yet the industry refuses to pay a better wage! Why? Because it's always been that way. Insanity! No wonder they can't afford to pay better interest rates on our savings accounts. It costs them too much to keep retraining these so-called important people.

If you have constant problems filling a tough position, reconfigure it to fit a wider berth of available talent—and pay better than the going rate. A few years ago a major fast-food chain lost millions of dollars—the result of a very successful toy giveaway promotion that cost them thousands of employees who quit from burnout and excessive hours as a result of the promotion. The loss was seen in additional training and recruiting costs. Hire talent and pay for what you expect.

Headhunters are not miracle workers.

Using four professional recruiters for one search is not the answer to filling a tough position.

Executive recruiters are bounty hunters, pure and simple. They sell time and contacts. They ride rainbows, look at the scenery, and decide where they want to get off and explore. Using a recruiter can be a terrific way to fill a difficult position, but you must commit to the assignment and feel confident in the recruiter.

Seasoned recruiters can smell a troubled company, indecisive managers, or a lame job from 3,000 miles, in a dense fog, while nursing an ear infection. Spend time educating a few proven search professionals on exactly what the job is and its potential. Consider investing in an engagement or retainer fee to encourage activity and prove you're serious about filling the spot. If you know the job is a no-win situation, consider reconfiguring the territory, abandoning the search altogether, or redefining the job to entice potential candidates.

Ask the search professional for a few references on recent and similar searches he or she has completed. This information will help you identify the recruiters who have many creative ideas but few resources to find and deliver the talent.

...you don't say?

Always do reference checks yourself.

Qualitative research has shown that more than 70 percent of hiring managers don't do reference checks. Frightening! Reference checks confirm impressions and educate you on how to motivate, train, and discipline the new hire. Reference checks extract pieces of personal information that can clarify a feeling or hunch you have of that person, saving you from making a bad hire. References typically compliment the potential employee, but good questions can elicit surprising and relevant information.

I called a reference who told me (thinking this would help the candidate) the candidate was a workaholic and had been known to abandon his family at parties to rush to the rescue at the plant. No offer was made.

Don't hire without making at least two reference checks *yourself.* If candidates claim they can't give any references for risk of their company finding out they're looking, don't hire them. Ever.

Cementing the hire...with chocolate?

*Flowers or a small gift to the spouse and
a solid offer is your best insurance against
a counteroffer being considered.*

Spouses of job candidates carry more influence than we imagine. They are sounding boards for your candidates. They make subtle observations and gain impressions from what the potential employees choose to tell them. If the opportunity is out of their comfort zone, spouses can deflate a deal in no time. A gift with a note helps put a caring person behind a cold offer letter and a lot of inconvenience. A phone call to the spouse is not a bad idea either (with the approval of the candidate, I suggest). However, pretty presents are not to be used to mask a weak offer or a job that won't be there after the first quarter.

Held for ransom

Never negotiate against a counteroffer. Never.

Once you make an offer to a candidate for employment and have negotiated it to the final number, that's it. Should the person come back with a comment, "Well, my current employer has offered to increase my pay, give me a promotion, and seal-coat my driveway for life, but I want to work for you. Is there any way you can match my company's offer?" Your response is simple and succinct: "No, we can't." You may feel like adding, "If you still want to work for them after you've blackmailed them into giving you *what we know you're worth, but they didn't have a clue until today,* then go ahead. And good luck." But don't say it!

Being held up for ransom is dangerous and manipulative. Don't look with disfavor just yet on your candidate for using this tactic. Many people get bad advice, feel guilty for quitting, are unsure of its fairness, or have a touch of buyer's remorse. Hold firm to your guns and wait for an answer. Eight out of ten times the candidate will come to work for you with this approach. If you have to sell a person on the opportunity too much, then you don't want the individual anyway.

Beyond a handshake deal

Always send a letter confirming your offer
of employment.

People forget. Put details in writing, and I mean *every-thing*. Offer letters also help future employees to re-sign their other job because they know your job offer is real; the job will actually be there after they have left their present position. Having a letter, something tangible, diminishes the appeal of counteroffers. People feel more commitment to you because you have put in writing, "We want you!"

Section IV

Managing & Retaining Sales Elite:
Easy for You to Stay!

*When you hire people who are smarter than you are,
you prove you are smarter than they are.*
—R. H. Grant

Feelin' good and feelin' wealthy

*Put intrinsic and extrinsic rewards in place
for all sales and management personnel.*

Thank-yous, employee of the month awards, achievement pins, commendation letters—all point to our deep inner need to feel appreciated and loved. Extrinsic rewards are increased income, a vacation won in a sales contest, a primo parking place for a great month, promotions—anything that is rewarded with financial or material gains. Without a blending of these two factors, salespeople will feel cheated and unsatisfied and leave sooner rather than later. And being able to provide each one when appropriate throughout the years gives you, the manager, opportunities to continually check and balance your sales team in both strong and weak business cycles.

Live and die by the 80/20 rule.

Prioritizing and targeting larger customers is crucial to keeping morale high and employees informed.

Vilfredo Pareto would have been a great sales manager. The late-nineteenth century, Italian sociologist formed an economic theory—the Pareto theory—that basically says 20 percent of your customers will account for 80 percent of your revenue, and 80 percent of sales made come from 20 percent of your sales force. Pull out your economics textbook and refamiliarize yourself with the 80/20 theory. The Web has over 100 sites on this subject. Remind your team that the same effort is expended on a big sale as a medium sale. Same components, same strategy, different pricing. Big sales are more productive. Small sales that are expensive to a small company attract lots of negotiating, deal making, and stalling. Walk away from these deals. Your staff will love you for it.

Observe big companies and watch them target certain customers to maximize their returns. Even if you own, run, or manage a small sales organization, there are things you can do to focus on more profitable business. Set minimum sales orders, seek advanced sales training programs, invest in market research to uncover customers that are bigger and in need of your products or services, raise the commission rate on larger orders, and see how quickly your orders get bigger overnight. Teach the staff you don't have to start at the bottom and work up. Be prepared to start at the top. Get a poster that has the 80/20 rule written on it, post it in your office, and see what happens.

Positive first impressions lead to sales.

Mandate that all sales personnel have professional selling tools in their briefcases: calculator; professional, good-looking writing implements; crisp brochures; and a laptop or weekly organizer of some kind. Burn any briefcase—in front of the home office— if it shows its owner lacks pride of ownership.

You may have the best product, service or people in the business, but customers will never know about it if they aren't motivated to continue a dialogue with your sales professionals. Remind sales personnel that the basics of grooming, neatness, and professionalism never go out of style. Time management is still in vogue in all business disciplines, so never stop preaching the gospel of being able to find information efficiently and looking sharp while you're doing it. Good business is a succession of simple things made to look crisp, sharp, and professional.

Overcoming technical denial

All personnel must be able to turn on a computer,
type, and print a letter. If not, they don't
go home until they can.

Pretty basic stuff, right? Make sure everybody can run a program. Even if your personnel are not equipped with laptops, they must know the basics. No exceptions.

Paperwork costs profit dollars.

Limit weekly reporting or logging-in time
to less than three hours per week.

Salespeople are action oriented. They like to keep busy selling and earning commissions. They're trained early that idle time is bad, that paperwork takes time away from selling and is unproductive. Consequently, you need to keep reporting methods to a minimum. Reconfigure your reporting systems to make them foolproof. Make it easy for them to contribute their data and get back out selling. Another option: hire a few lower-salaried administrators to input data rather than use talented salespeople to do it.

Visit the mine so you don't get the shaft.

Keep outside salespeople in touch with corporate planning and direction. The independence of sales personnel is critical, but it can breed detachment.

Home-based salespeople need interaction with the boss. They are the real gold of the business—the lifeline and profit link to attracting new customers. They need assurance, feedback, and someone to bounce personal and business issues off of. Without this interaction, they can become distracted, isolated, and frustrated in their jobs. Spending a day with them, dining with them, visiting their family, giving them a forum to air their thoughts and get your advice is the best use of your time as a manager. Find a way to meet them a few times a quarter to maintain continuity and steady performance as well as to diagnose any problems.

Journey to the center of the girth

*Offer an $800 yearly health club allowance and an
$800 continuing education allowance.
Make it a "use it or lose it" policy.*

Yes, people should stay fit, stop smoking, reduce alcohol consumption, learn to control stress and consume less fats, but not all of us do. Sometimes we just need a nudge in the pudge to get started. And yes, we should all be lifetime learners, but that too is easier said than done. Encourage your team to take time to practice healthy activities and challenge their minds. They may resist at first, but if you set an example, it may turn them around. Don't forget to let your sales professionals know that if they choose not to use these allowances they'll be explaining why they haven't to you.

Schedule your next meeting at a Blockbuster Video store.

Who knows what ideas will come up when you think outside the box.

Meeting at a Blockbuster store or any other unusual venue does great things for creative thinking and team building. Boardrooms and meeting rooms stifle creative thinking through lack of stimuli. At Blockbuster, serve popcorn and Milk Duds and let the ideas flow! Try this when you have a chance to meet offsite.

Now, class,
here's the extra-credit portion...

Establish "extra credit" for special projects.
Create a list of ten new business ventures or product/
service ideas. The "takers" are your next managers.

Those individuals who go above and beyond the call of duty will become the best managers. The top salesperson who doesn't go after different projects or offer help in other areas will not usually excel as a sales manager. Look for the hand raisers and curiosity seekers. The world of sports teaches that successful head coaches were not always the superstars during their playing days.

The bottom line is: how much will I earn?

Commission plans must be understandable without a scientific calculator. Simplify them to show your sales reps how wealthy they can become.

A sales professional should be able to estimate—in the customer's parking lot, on a piece of paper—what his commission will be if he or she makes that particular sale. Simplifying commission plans is the first step to educating sales professionals to use their time for bigger sales and not waste time on futile deals. Salespeople are motivated by money, as well as by the need to persuade; if you give them fuel to fire up both these emotions, they will perform far better than they themselves ever expected.

Golden handcuffs for newcomers

*Create a "Retention Bonus Club:" A percentage
of the employee's compensation to be paid
after three to four years of employment.*

When a worldwide manufacturing conglomerate I was working for was having high turnover in their sales ranks, they elected to conduct a simple experiment. They announced a stay bonus equal to one year's salary if a person was with them four years starting from the moment the opportunity was announced. The result? Turnover did recede, and curiously, performance of the salespeople increased.

It could be hypothesized that the salespeople wanted to ensure they didn't get fired before the big payout date, with the result being increased sales revenue and a re-energized team. The increased sales more than paid for the stay bonuses and made it difficult for competitors to lure their people away with the almighty buck. (Interestingly enough, one of the sales managers who was thinking of quitting before the stay bonus was introduced decided to stay for a while. Four years later the company was for sale and he, along with four other executives, bought the company, making him even more money. And they still paid out the bonuses to the people who had earned them prior to the sale.)

Paying out $10,000 to a proven sales rep or manager after three or four years of employment is a lot cheaper than replacing that person after two years. Golden handcuffs do work, and they work both for the long and short term. Placing a financial incentive will keep good people longer, as long as the management team is fair, honest, and progressive. Money can't buy you loyalty, but it will buy you consistent performance in sales, as well as time to fix any internal glitches you've discovered. Advertising the program in the company newsletter and promotional pieces to the general public isn't a bad idea either.

This joke's on you.

Laugh it up!

Has your staff seen you laugh in the past few days? Too busy to laugh? Are business demands so intense that it's difficult to see humor in a situation? Are you concerned your chuckles may indicate vulnerability and a weak presence in the business community? Hogwash. People are skeptical of persons who don't have a sense of humor. Laughing is a universal language, a sign of acceptance and spontaneous feeling and emotions. It is a tension reliever and offers a big breather in a big meeting. Sitcoms on TV even have to encourage us to laugh with laugh tracks. It's as if some of us need written permission to giggle. You will attract and retain staff far longer with humor and sincere efforts than with an iron fist. I heard of a president who purposely sat on a whoopee cushion at a meeting to ease the tension.

Do you dare?

Excuse me, but that's my nose, not the pencil sharpener.

Hold sales meetings in tight quarters.
Closeness encourages interaction.

Attention assured managers! Never sit at the head of the table. Park yourself right in the middle. Invite others to sit closer to you and change the mix of who sits where. This ain't church. Move around. Break stale habits. I worked at a company where the two big shots always sat at opposing ends of a long conference table. This way a person couldn't see the reaction of one of the big shots, so the big shots could subtly communicate secretly in the same meeting. It was like watching a tennis match from three feet, trying to talk to both of them. The result was frustrating and confusing meetings. The tighter the space, the more ideas take place. Big tables, big rooms, and wide berths breed quiet and reserved dialogue. Close together, sharing food, passing stuff to each other, mingling with management does wonders for good communication, faster meetings, and a better exchange of ideas.

High goals, high pay, high company earnings

Create an incentive plan to allow salespersons
to earn more than 50 percent of their salary
when they attain some doable but tough numbers.
And don't lower the base salary either.

Want to find out if a new product is going to make it in the market? Give the sales team big commission dollars to sell it and watch what happens. Federal Express told us that waiting five days for a package was foolish, but we didn't think about it until they mentioned it. If there's a market, motivated sales professionals will uncover the needs better than any marketing or focus group can. The extra commissions you pay out will more than recoup any losses you had in research that told you "maybe it'll sell, maybe not."

Hold your next sales meeting in the hall.

You'll probably resolve most issues there anyway.
Try holding meetings in the bathroom,
if you want more privacy than the hall.

It's happened to all of us at some point. We realize the formal meetings are corporate cheerleading drills staged for the shareholders or the marketing people to show off the new ideas with much fanfare. Your time is valuable and there's no need to be there for eight hours, so you finish your business in the hall in fifteen minutes. Why not hold your next meeting there? People think faster on their feet. They appreciate the value of time. Try this when you need to hold a meeting on the premises. See what happens.

It's 11:00 P.M. Do you know where your customers are?

Sales reps should have with them at all times the home phone numbers of the main contacts of their top ten accounts.

Throughout my sixteen years of recruiting sales and management talent, I have found the majority of these professionals can't put their hands on this critical data without a lot of digging. The 80/20 rule that says 80 percent of your business comes from 20 percent of your customers still hasn't hit home with them. The ability to connect with your top customers at a moment's notice for business or personal banter is the difference between a "long-term" and a "not any more" customer. If your people don't have the information handy, they're probably not working with them enough.

Cast away, lad, into the great wide open.

Mandate a three-week sabbatical every two years for sales managers. No phone calls allowed. No exceptions.

New ideas come while people are sitting on tractors, lying on beaches, hiking mountains, hitting the par-five in two, shopping in Paris, building a screened porch, antique hunting in Maine, or wandering the castles of Scotland. Reward sales managers with free time—paid, of course—to do nothing but have fun. No rules, no suggestions. They must simply disappear to a place where you can't find them. It's amazing what ideas they'll come back with as well as a heightened sense of loyalty to you and to the company.

I personally find that if I don't take a few long vacations throughout the year, I'm not as good as I should be. A grouch, basically. I get shades of self-importance, ("the world won't run right if I'm not here to hold the wheel"), or I get greedy, worrying about missing some piece of business. These feelings dissipate with R & R. I find that the business doesn't go away; if anything, more comes to me if I give clients some breathing room. It also shows them I'm confident and secure enough in my life to take time away, that I care about my health, my family.

Go on, tell me. I can take it.

*Create a "customer evaluate us" form
and pass it out by next Monday.*

There's a lot of talk about value-added service these days, though the majority of companies don't poll their customers on a regular basis. Make today the day for your company and your customers. What you find out will surprise you, scare you, thrill you, anger you, and motivate you to do things differently when you get up tomorrow.

Trash your favorite, beat-up slippers.

Effective immediately: 15 percent
of yearly sales must be "new business," uncovered
within the last twelve months. Next year: 20 percent.

New, clean business increases profits. Old, established business keeps the machines running and inventory going out the door, but old business is done at a lower price and with old expectations. And old business goes away some day; you just don't know when. Assertive business development is insurance that you won't get blindsided by established customers taking business elsewhere. Sales professionals must be "incentivized" to grow business. Maintaining customers can be achieved with good internal support or periodic visits. Buy yourself a new pair of slippers to protect your feet from the chilly reality that business must always be pursued.

...and the winner is...

*Create a "Nobel prize" for the top two
or three ideas of the year.*

I've witnessed sales contests during which people have worked five and ten hours a week extra to win a $200 television, whereas the same energy exerted in non-contest periods would have earned them $20,000 in additional income! Given this wacky phenomenon, contests are great motivators and stimulators of teamwork and creativity. Have a few prize months per year and watch the sparks fly!

It's midnight. Do you know who else knows where your customers are?

Do you know the names and locations of your top seven competitors? Stop reading and find out now.

More than 60 percent of the candidates on the market today who sell or manage don't know this fact. Test it out at your next sales meeting. It's amazing how brilliant sales professionals can sound in front of a customer when they know all about the competitors' strengths and weaknesses. Sometimes a perceived competitor is really not a competitor. Find out exactly what they can and can't do compared to your firm's ability. Invest two days or have an assistant track down this data and share it with the team. Better yet, hold a contest among the sales team—the one with the best data wins a getaway weekend to somewhere exotic.

If you build it, they'll read from it.

Create a Library of Achievement.

Buy the top twenty sales training books, tapes, and videos on the market and keep them in your office for your sales team to use. Have an assistant administer the checking in and out process. Having a library that rotates the best material on selling throughout your sales force will do wonders toward enhancing sales, building team spirit, customer satisfaction, and building wealth for you and your sales professionals. Start with some of the best authors: Denis Waitley, Ken Blanchard, Tom Peters, Zig Ziglar, Neil Rackham, Peter Drucker, Warren Bennis, Harvey Mackay, Stephan Covey or Brian Tracy. Contact Nightingale-Conant Corporation, in Chicago, for their catalog; they're the largest producer and distributor of sales training and motivational audiocassettes and CDs in the world.

"Mr. Toobusy...please pick up the white courtesy phone. Paging Mr. Toobusy."

All calls to you from a sales rep in the field should be returned within two hours.

If you're the boss and they can't get your attention, they'll leave to be appreciated somewhere else. Arrogance, claims of being "too busy," won't cut it as an excuse to leave a sales professional without a call. Tolerate no excuses from lack of promptness of your sales team, your management team, or yourself. Statistics show the majority of sales professionals don't leave because of money, but because of *perceived* lack of appreciation and respect from their boss.

Show me the money!

Inquire about the existence of a savings or retirement plan for every salesperson and manager in your group.

Sadly, a high percentage of Americans do not have a regular, systematic savings program. Even corporate dollar-matching 401(k)s are not used by all workers. Sit down with your sales team as a group or individually and explain the value of such things as compound interest, 401(k)s, stock plans, mutual funds, and certificates of deposit (CDs). Help them appreciate the feeling of having some money in the bank. Hire a financial consultant for the day to speak with your team on investing and financial programs. (You may even find a good one for free if the person is given the chance to work with the employees in the financial investing.) Set employees' sights on financial independence. Show them what they can do if they earn more: lifestyle changes, vacations, opening up their own business someday after they've outgrown their existing job. You can be a hero to people who have never received any coaching on the topic of investing.

"That's a nice suit.
Does it come in your size?"

Hire an image consultant for the day.

In the past fifteen years, my coworkers have cut two neckties from my neck and they've seen to it that one of my coats disappeared. They were right in doing it, too. For less than $500, you can teach your staff how to dress for success. Most people never are taught how to dress effectively for business, the appropriateness of certain clothing, or what colors and styles flatter a person's physique. It will make a difference. It will make a statement to your team that you're committed to hiring the best, and having the best look their best.

Park the pink Cadillac out back.

Remove all reserved parking,
except for visitors and handicapped.

Reserve the space for the top salesperson of the month, the person who had the best idea of the week, or the limousine to take the group to lunch after a great quarter. Status symbols are great to *give*, not to show off to the team. People work harder for you if you reward them, not intimidate them.

Naked paper

Try business cards without titles for twelve months.

Everybody is a salesperson. See if people ask you what your title is. If you're asking enough of the right questions and doing the job right, customers won't care and won't have time to ask. It shows your team that you're all in it together. It'll be interesting to see what people call themselves when they pick their own titles and job descriptions.

To belch or not to belch:
that is the question.

Take them all to international etiquette school for a day.

D o you know how to accept a business card from a Japanese businessman? Did you just toss your gum out the window in Taiwan? Uh-oh. Would you know if you just offended a foreign customer at lunch by *not* belching? Spend a day with a consultant specializing in international business and etiquette training. Most of the major corporations in America provide some form of training for their employees who travel abroad. And fortunately, it's not expensive. A consultant for a full day could be less than $1,500. That's a bargain! One *faux pas* at lunch or at the negotiation table could cost you much more. This type of progressive thinking speaks volumes to your team about being the best, as well as showing respect for clients by attempting to learn and understand their customs and traditions.

Short-term means long-term and long-term means short-term.

All sales personnel in your organization should have an attainable incentive plan from day one. If they don't, then don't call them sales professionals.

Convincing a salesperson to put out effort with the promise of a big payoff is crazy. From day one a professional salesperson has to see a carrot and trust that it won't disappear when he or she reaches it. As companies continue to merge, spin off, rightsize, supersize, you name it, sales professionals will not become top performers without a big-bang potential. The future is now. Future incentives don't hold the interest of sales professionals, and skepticism will keep promises of the future in the bottom drawer. The sooner you reward, the sooner the goals will be achieved. The shorter the time it takes to make the payoff goals, the longer the employee will stay with you and sell, sell, sell.

Required reading:
SPIN SELLING by Neil Rackham

*Have your employees read and commit to memory
the sales strategies from the best sales strategy-
training book on the market.*

As an employer, you have the right to expect your staff to read anything you ask them to, within reason. Everybody needs to be on the same page when it comes to customer contact, selling skills, and performance reviews. The book *SPIN SELLING* is a great way to get people's minds moving in the same direction, creating a positive attitude toward the customer contact process.

Wash the front windows.

*Cleaning the house before company
comes over shows respect.*

How does the front door of your building look? Is it clean and fresh? Is the plant in order, clean and sparkling, showing pride of ownership? Does your desk look like you work at it or use it as a storage area? Does your company car look like a rolling storage locker? Is the lobby inviting, or a place to store old chairs and save old magazines? First impressions ring true still. Cut the grass yourself if you have to—imagine the impression you'll make!

The pitch-it party

Throw out any excess papers, files, junk, and furniture.
Donate it or burn it and take pictures
for the company newsletter.

F act: The law, yes the law, mandates that when our new president of the United States moves into the White House, it must be immaculate. No papers, file folders, paper clips, Post-it Notes, not even crumbs from a bagel are to be left behind. Why? So things don't get more mixed up than they already are! We could all use a dose of this cleanup policy in our basements and garages. But for now, practice it at the office and celebrate the open space. You may even uncover a business lead that slipped through the cracks!

Musical chairs

Everybody changes places for a day or for one meeting.

How would you react if the boss changed the commission plan in midyear, and it cost you big bucks? You probably wouldn't be too happy. As the boss, you know material costs have risen 49 percent in two months, so to offset the costs you need to cut the auto allowance, overtime pay, and reduce air travel for your technicians. But how would your employees know that? Put people in different positions for a day to "walk a mile in the other person's shoes." If you let others know the issues you face, they will be less apt to criticize and more likely to accept decisions that affect their lives. This kind of openness builds a real team.

Let go of the leash.

*Eliminate regular weekly meetings for the staff. If you
need to gather the flock for a count, you lack trust in the
group and it shows. Let them sell or let them go.*

Rah-rah meetings are dinosaur tactics. Motivating a
person to achieve a specific objective is accomplished by a one-on-one approach to evaluation of
goals and objectives. A synergistic approach will help the
employee to focus on activities that lead to his or her goal.
Motivational speeches and seminars are great, but is it re-
alistic to think a person can sustain the excitement long after the initial "high"? True, highs and lows in selling are always present. Helping a person to manage these emotions
is hard to do, but even harder with team meetings. Instead, use this time to outline individual programs for your
team. The results will be greater than gathering the masses
just to count the sheep.

Accountability day

December 15: Every salesperson turns in a resume.

What better way to see in print what your group has done? Writing a resume forces them to prove they've actually been working the past year. It's a great exercise to help marginal performers reach new levels and let superstars set higher goals and prove they're ready to be promoted. It gives a wake-up call to those who just won't make the cut to start looking for another job.

By encouraging your people to write their resume, you are really building loyalty and a positive environment, demonstrating your courage and willingness to help them advance or improve. Salespeople will leave at some point regardless of what you do or how much you pay. Helping the individual prosper and look good on paper is rewarded with loyalty and a desire to improve performance. And by the way, don't forget to write your own resume!

Philanthropy for the amateur

*Provide a philanthropic budget of $200 to $500
per year for all salespeople having more than half
a million dollars in sales revenue. Allow them
to choose the charity and give the money
in their name as well as the company's.*

Benevolence is very rewarding. Giving your employees the opportunity to experience the heartwarming feeling of giving to others goes a long way toward developing their "charity consciousness." It also speaks highly of your firm's commitment to humanitarian issues. Even a small amount of money can make a difference somewhere, and you'll be promoting the practice for others to follow. Philanthropy is not reserved for the rich; it is an equal opportunity action.

Section V

Staying Sharp

The key to becoming successful is to work harder on yourself than on your job.
—Jim Rohn

"...because we've always done it that way."

Bring a novice to your business for a day to follow you around and ask "why" in response to everything you do.

Hanging around people your own age, with similar tastes, similar incomes, and similar houses breeds stale thinking and boring parties. Invite your gardener, pharmacist, general contractor—anybody you know but don't hang around with—to your house for dinner or to your office for a few hours. Pay them to ask silly and obvious questions. They'll see things you don't see. They'll wonder what you do all day and you'll have to tell them. And maybe you'll find out you're not doing something you should be!

Hello? Anybody home?

*Personally contact any customer who was
doing business with your firm a year ago
but is not doing so today.*

If you're the boss or a sales professional new to the office, calling former customers can bring healing to those relationships. Letting customers vent their frustrations, disappointments, whatever, can help you reconnect with them if you want to. Customers go away for a lot of silly and vague reasons and for some very serious and unchangeable reasons. Finding out why they left and wooing them back is worth a week's worth of calls around the holidays. Try it.

Never stop seeing customers.

Out of sight, out of business.

W hether you own the place in hometown USA or run a global sales force, visit with customers. Let them see your commitment to their needs. Don't do your sales team's job, just visit. Encourage your sales team to invite you with them, but promise them you won't interfere. The sales professional is the CEO of a sales call.

Whose turn is it to tell
the emperor he's naked?

*Question intensely any salesperson working for you
who doesn't personally object to at least one of your
decisions per year. No top performer is that content,
and no manager is that right all the time.*

You're good, but not perfect. Meet with each person,
assuring him or her that all comments will be kept in
confidence and you desire to learn from this experience. What can you do to help him or her? What do you
do that drives the person crazy? What policies stink?
Which are outdated? What stifles creativity or the ability to
sell more? The individual will tell you the answers if the
spirit of the meeting is upbeat and if you are approachable. If you don't hear anything negative, you may be too
intimidating. Time to take a personal day and figure out
what you can do to become approachable.

Of course, I'll buy 150 more boxes.

Feel guilty not buying cookies from the Girl Scout at your front door? Read Influence: The Psychology of Persuasion *by Robert B. Cialdini, Ph.D.*

This book, written more than ten years ago, is a perennial top seller and a must-read for any sales manager. The book explores and dissects why and how humans process influencing behavior in all personal, social, and business settings. You will be amazed to learn just how simple and intimidating it is to influence people for good and bad. Read it before you read this Sunday's paper.

Buy copies for your sales team and management and make the book required reading. Discuss it at your next sales meeting—in the hallway, of course. And pass out the cookies you bought from a great salesperson: the Girl Scout.

What were those words to live by?

Be able to recite your personal and professional philosophy.

Every mentor you have ever met has a set of standards he or she abides by. Call it a philosophy, laws of living, creed, rules, dogmas—whatever the label, it is a deep, strong thread woven into the fabric of his or her character. You remember these people as long as you live. They challenge you, encourage you, stretch your mind, hold you accountable, let you sweat. They give you room to risk, to live, to excel. Make sure your own philosophy is apparent in your persona; it is this energy and value system that attracts the top businesspeople to you and your organization. A great book to read on this subject is *The Seven Habits of Highly Effective People* by Stephen Covey. His analysis of morals, ethics, energy management, and personal development is easy to read but packed with a wealth of material that will motivate you to change for the better. Don't leave home without it—a living philosophy, that is.

Volunteerism

Live your philosophy of business by helping others.

People judge a book by the cover at first, but the first three pages will determine whether the book actually gets read. Volunteerism is a tremendous way to show gratitude and give back to the community. It refreshes the soul and refuels our faith in mankind's willingness to help his neighbor. It is a noble effort and is rewarding without receiving monetary or material gifts.

But having said this, I must add that volunteerism is a simple way to reach out in the community to attract like-minded individuals. Those who volunteer are well respected in the community. They get their pictures in the newspaper, newsletters, annual reports, and promotional pieces. Would you like these people on your team? Would they want you, a caring volunteer, as their leader? You bet. Fund-raisers, car washes, paint-a-thons, lake cleanup projects, cookie sales, pancake breakfasts, parade judging, sign painting, reading for the blind, church ushers—all contribute to our sanity and demonstrate our willingness to help. Even if we have intentions beyond the purely altruistic, the fact is we are helping those in need.

What will life be like after business?

Planning is great, but the thrill
of business is all about the moment.

The clichés are endless with reference to living in the moment, the most famous one being "I never heard anybody on their deathbed saying they wished they'd spent more time at the office." I have a good friend, a CEO, who at age fifty is starting to plan for a reduced work schedule by taking one week of vacation extra every year. He believes this approach will lessen the stress and increase his enjoyment of retirement or a less than forty-hour workweek.

All too often executives push themselves and their businesses to the limit in their work life. If they decide to call it quits, get fired, lose a political battle, or whatever, the transition to less than 100 mph is extremely stressful and psychologically challenging. Peter Drucker, author and total quality management guru, talks of the need to begin to plan the second half of your life before you arrive. Begin to find hobbies and activities, worthy opportunities to volunteer, or a new business venture now. It gives you time to reflect and ease the strain of having to quit and go into a strange new world—a world of not working sixty hours a week.

In the meantime enjoy the thrill of the marketplace right now. Celebrate the big deal now. Rejoice in having attained the promotion now, instead of immediately looking at the next rung of your endless ladder that may be leaning against the wrong wall. Smile on your success and imagine how you'll feel looking back on this time knowing you did your best.

Controlling growth—
in more ways than one

*Consistency in business practices and personal health
are vital to healthy organizations and organs.*

Patience is a virtue that all motivated business professionals would love to have, but not have to practice unless required by law. We want to make it happen now, close the deal now, grow the territory now, pay off debt now, hire more people now. And growth is good. To a point. Growth without adequate preparation, without advance notice to your "soon to be overwhelmed" staff, without analyzing the business from all angles, can be disastrous, to say the least.

The number one goal of any corporation is to make a profit, but that doesn't mean a business has to grow in sales volume to generate a profit. Controlled growth, securing solid, profitable business (remember Pareto's 80/20 rule) is superior to keeping the machines humming with low profit margin business that chokes machine time. Are you growing methodically, in a reasonable state of chaos? Do you have an advisory board—formal or informal—to bounce these issues off of?

112

And what about your physical growth? Yes, you. How's your health throughout all this? Is your waistline growing faster than the company's bottom line? Are you focused on maintaining your personal fitness to ensure you'll be around to cash in or cash out? Will you be able to do the things you've talked about doing in retirement or that "slower business schedule" with your current fitness regimen? If not, now is the time to rethink priorities and set examples. Promoting a fit company while being an unfit specimen sends mixed signals to employees, shareholders, and family members. (Have you noticed? You rarely see an overweight CEO of a Fortune 500 organization. There's a reason for this.)

Self-analysis time

How are you doing with all this stuff?

Managing people is difficult. The challenges of sorting out people's personal issues, business aspirations, social issues, and expectations of corporate profits are hard to balance. Time and energy are two valuable commodities to any manager. All too often, your personal time and energy suffer because of job pressures. Finding a happy medium to balance life's tugs of family, fitness, work, financial obligations, and chasing dreams warrants decisions to be made that don't always please everybody. Are you taking enough time for yourself to grow? Are you keeping your business skills sharp and updated? Are you being fair and honest with your expectations of what work gives you, or better yet, what you expect from your employees? Have you taken a vacation with your family recently? Did you have fun? Did you call in to the office?

Succeeding in business is quite simple if we clearly define the basics of how to service the customer and how to treat others, but emotions tip us upside down, making it tough to do the right thing. Be willing to risk being the first one to try something in your organization. If you're good at what you do, it will work out fine. Even if it doesn't work, you'll have a better idea of what will work next time. Pick a few ideas a month to work on that seem to strike a chord in you. Promise yourself to do something different this week to make yourself better, smarter, happier, challenged, richer, more valuable. Write your own resume—your own ticket to succeed in any pursuit you feel compelled and passionate enough to undertake.

About the Author

Russell J. Riendeau has been an executive search professional since 1985. He's the senior partner of The East Wing Group in Barrington, Illinois. His first book, *Thinking on Your Seat*, is a guide for those wishing to enter the field of executive recruitment. He is a nationally recognized speaker and trainer for recruiting excellence and peak performance. Riendeau's ideas and writings have appeared in the *Wall Street Journal, Sales & Marketing Management, Selling Magazine*, and Nightingale-Conant's Audio Program. Prior to entering the recruitment business, he spent nine years as a homebuilder.

Riendeau holds a master's degree in developmental psychology and is a candidate for a Ph.D. in psychology. He lives with his wife and two children in Barrington, Illinois.

Please send:

_____copies of *Finders Keepers*
at $9.95 each   TOTAL   _____

Nebr. residents add 5% sales tax   _____

Shipping/Handling
    $4.00 for first book.
    $1.00 for each additional book.   _____

        TOTAL ENCLOSED   _____

Name _____

Address _____

City_____State ____Zip_____

    ☐   Visa   ☐   Master Card   ☐   Am. Express

Credit card number _____

Expiration date _____

Order by credit card, personal check or money order.
Send to:

Addicus Books
Mail Order Dept.
P.O. Box 45327
Omaha, NE 68145
Or, order **TOLL FREE:** 800-352-2873
online at www.AddicusBooks.com